The Complete Book of Australian Verse

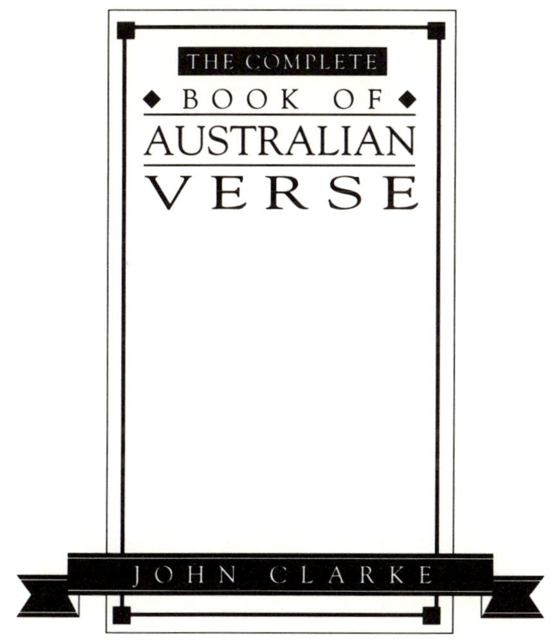

Illustrations by Jenny Coopes

A Susan Haynes book

Allen & Unwin Australia
Sydney Wellington London Boston

For Helen

Illustrations by Jenny Coopes

First published in 1989

A Susan Haynes book
Allen & Unwin Australia Pty Ltd
An Unwin Hyman Company
8 Napier Street, North Sydney, NSW 2060, Australia

Allen & Unwin New Zealand Limited
75 Ghuznee St, Wellington, New Zealand

Unwin Hyman Limited
15-17 Broadwick Street, London WIV IFP, England

Allen & Unwin Inc.
8 Winchester Place, Winchester, Mass 01890, USA

National Library of Australia
Cataloguing-in-publication

Clarke, John, 1948-
The complete book of Australian verse.
ISBN 0 04 301295 7.
I. Coopes, Jenny. II. Title.
A821'.3

Designed by P.A.G.E. Pty Ltd
Set in Goudy by P.A.G.E. Pty Ltd

Printed in Singapore by South Wind Productions

Contents

Introduction

For many years it was assumed that poetry came from England. Research now clearly demonstrates, however, that a great many of the world's most famous poets were actually Australians. Works by major poets have been discovered in various parts of Australia and are published here for the first time. This collection aims to put on record the wealth of imagery and ideas in Australian verse.

English is a language relatively new to Australia and obviously in a nation so young there can be no Icelandic Sagas, no Chaucer, and no Shakespeare[1]. Certain other works have been tragically lost. The great Neville Shelley of Eildon , for instance, survives only in the oral tradition[2]. Ewen Coleridge, the so-called 'Automatic Writer', left nothing whatever and Stumpy Byron V.C.[3] has not been included because so much of his work was written in Greece and Italy. It is virtually impossible to find anything from Brian Browning[4] or from 'Shagger' Tennyson, who refused point blank to write anything down.

In other respects, however, this is the most complete collection of Australian verse ever published.

Such an anthology would not be possible were it not for the kind assistance of the poets, their descendants or executors. I would also thank Ms. Lurleen Hopcroft for her work in typing the manuscripts and for her tireless support and cheerful presence.

---

[1] Although fragments have been found around Stratford near Horsham, of a work beginning 'Would there be any point in my drawing some sort of comparison between yourself and an absolute scorcher?'

[2] 'Pommymandius' can still be heard in pubs but no authentic manuscript exists.

[3] Stumpy Byron V.C. Best-known for swimming at night across the shark-infested Dardanelles in order to light fires on unoccupied beaches and confuse the Turks. The Victoria Cross was awarded posthumously since Stumpy caught the 'flu and died a few weeks later.

[4] Brian Browning, poet and cricket lover. Rumoured to have seen every Test Match played in Australia between 1922 and 1939. Best known for the work beginning 'Oh to be in April now that England's here'.

Bob Herrick

A Boer War veteran who passed away some years back, Bob is well remembered by local church-people in the Mittagong area, where he lived and worked.

Upon Julia's Speedos

Whenas in Speedos Julia goes,
Their fabric seemeth to expose
The wonders it doth juxtapose!

Next, when I cast mine eyes and see,
That lycra stretching each way free,
Tumescence overtaketh me!

Bill Blake

The late Bill Blake, rebel, painter and engraver, was a seasonal rabbiter who only dabbled in poetry until finishing runner-up in New Faces with The Book of Thel. After that, there was no holding him and many of his works are now among the most familiar in the language.

The Work of Harmony

Whose hobs are these, whose forging shape?
What metal wrought? What noble ape
With mighty arm in clamour raises
What the bellows? What the blazes?
Is it truly thee Oh Lord,
Whose alchemy transmutes the sward?
Or is the serpent active yet?
The cygnet and the leveret
Have robed in joy and innocence,
The beauty of thy congruence.

'Tim'rous' Howard – silhouette by an unknown artist.

Rabbi Burns

The son of poor farmers, Rabbi Burns became well known for poems in the regional dialect of The Mallee.

To A Howard

Wee, sleekit, cowerin, tim'rous beastie,
I know tha's probably doing thy bestie,
But the kind'st heart wuid ha' to see
Thou's nay made a fist o' the thing,
For e'en when there's nothin at a' to say
And ye'd far better tak to th' hills fo' th' day
Tha opens thy gob a' the drop o' the noo
And thou lets the wind bloo tha tongue aroon.

Och ye poor wee laddie, ye've no got the breen,
Ye've no got the sense to come oot o' the reen,
Why don't thou gi'e it awa' and gae hame,
It's no guid th' watch if ye can't tell th' tame,
There are jobs gang aplenty awa' at the farm
Afrightening birds by waving th' arms,
Ye ken they're gae keen t' employ the bold laddies
Awa' at the links where they're lookin for caddies,
If that's no to thy taste and thou's wanting a change
Thou'll try wi' th' gunnery up at the range,
Thou'll no have much truible, thou've dun it afore,
Thou's an expert for a' that; look, 'Wanted: Small Bore'.

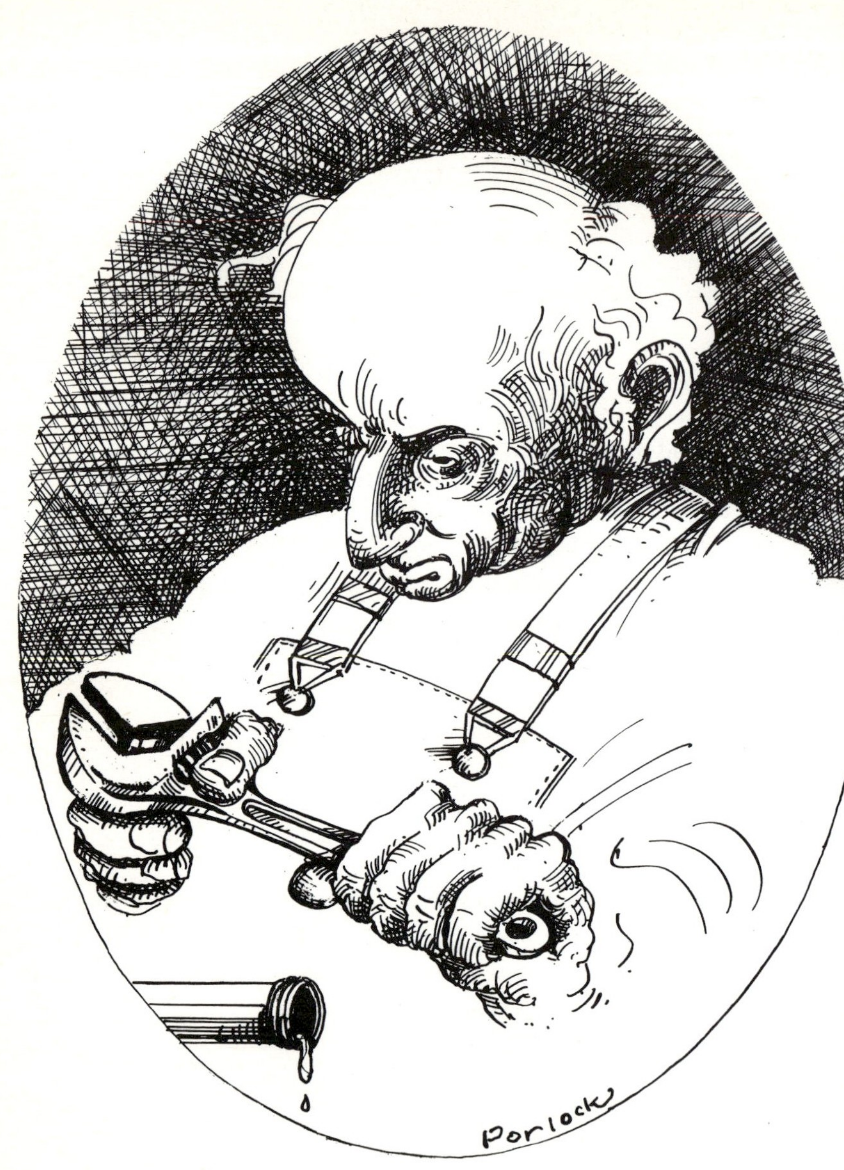

A. Wordsworth – a contemporary etching probably by J.S. Porlock.

Arnold Wordsworth

Arnold Wordsworth was a plumber in Sydney during the first half of the 19th century and was responsible for much of the underground piping in Annandale and Balmain. He lived with his sister Gail and with his mate Ewen Coleridge, who shared his interest in plumbing, poetry and Gail.

Lines Composed About Half-way Across the Pyrmont Bridge

Earth has not anything to show more fair,
Soft would he be of swede, a quid unfull,
Who would willingly forgo such a view,
For lo, the sparrow breaketh of his wind
And this entire joint looks not too foul,
Stand back, for when she goes, she bloody goes.

Trevor Henry Leigh Hunt

When 'Jenny Hit Me' was first published in 1838, Trevor Henry Leigh Hunt ran 'The Examiner' and knew almost everyone in Australia. A friend of Stumpy Byron V.C., Neville Shelley and Jay Esmill, he also supported Warren Keats and 'Shagger' Tennyson when they were getting going. He did two years in Long Bay for criticising a lobster in a Sydney restaurant.

Jenny Hit Me

Jenny hit me when we met,
   Leaping from the knee she sat on;
Fate, you clown, who love to get
   Medals on your chest, pin that on!
Say I'm ancient, say I'm mad,
   Say the costume doesn't fit me,
Say that Santa drinks, but add,
   Jenny hit me.

Thomas Wolfe

Possibly not a poet of the first rank, but related on his mother's side to two members of the Literature Board, one of whom is a Publisher and the other an Arts Advisor to the Bicentennial. Wolfe wrote approximately four poems and now lives in Tuscany.

The Burial of Surgeon Moore at Narrunga

Not a drum was heard, not a funeral note
As his mortal remains we carried,
From the secret laboratory round to his house
To the woman to whom he was married.

'Begging your pardon,' we said to his wife,
'Your husband appears to have carked it,
We've brought all his papers and tapers and things
And the ute is outside where he parked it.

There's nothing unsafe about nuclear testing,
Be perfectly clear about that,
He might have said otherwise but he was wrong,
Here, look at the hole in his hat.'

A. ROSE is A. ROSE is A. ROSE

Warren Keats

An unashamedly modern poet whose interest is in marrying classical forms with contemporary themes. Warren's promise is limitless if he can beat the grog.

A Customary Tale

There was a naughty boy
And a naughty boy was he,
He wandered up to Bangkok
The people for to see—
There he saw
That a whore
Was as pretty,
That a fight
Was as hitty,
That a kilo
Was as sold,
That a jail
Was as cold,
That a bribe
Was as taken,
That for
Was as saken,
That a lie
Was as sworn,
That a sucker
Was as born
Every minute—
So he sat in the dock
And he wonder'd
He wonder'd
He sat in the dock
And he wonder'd.

Fifteen Bobsworth Longfellow

Fifteen Bobsworth Longfellow was an Adelaide academic who wrote instructions for kit-set model products, mainly balsa wood aircraft and submarines which ran on baking powder. The manual included here was for the assembling of a 25 foot Aircraft Carrier marketed by Myer stores between 1954 and 1960.

Myer's Whopper

Take the pieces from the package,
Lay them out as per the graph,
Gathering the bits you'll need,
Removing what you shouldn't have.
With the implement provided
Ease the bearings to the left,
Push the little angled mullion
Up into the socket 'F'.
This will free the moulded bracket
Holding back the nylon strand,
Draw the slippery hoop and coupling
Through the right-hand rubber-band.
Put the topside brown side outside,
Push the inside upside down,
Underneath the left-hand wingnut,
Press the folding backward crown.
Overlapping lifting side-flaps
Lower in to fit the screws,
Pack up tools, retire to distance,
Don protective hat, light fuse.

Ted Lear

Ted Lear popularised Limericks in his 'A Book of Rubbish', although tragically he failed to recognise that the way to make them work was to have a filthy last line.

Limericks

There was an old man with a beard,
A funny old man with a beard,
He had a big beard,
A great big old beard,
That amusing old man with a beard.

There once was a woman whose hat,
Was a regular brute of a hat,
Oh a hat she did wear,
On the top of her hair,
And everyone said 'Look! A hat!'

There was an old fellow from Bong,
Who hailed in the first place from Bong,
From Bong did he come,
With Bongolian rum,
That humorous old fellow from Bong.

There was an old man with a bird,
Who was an old man with a bird,
The bird with the man,
Confessed 'It's absurd
I'm the bird with the man with the bird!'

Marianne More

Born near Broken Hill, Marianne More has always had a feeling for the expanse and majesty of Australia and the natural world. She went to school in Adelaide.

The Majesty of Great Big Animals

The majesty of bison as they roam,
Is awesome, in the North, in spring, I've seen,
The majesty of lizards, and observed,
The majesty of easy climbing birds,
Whose majesty is manifest in groups.

The trees are in their awesome beauty now,
Majestic kangaroos abound in scores,
And groups of birds lift lazily and wheel,
Like lazy groups of wheeling birds aloft,
Especially near a river, did you ever
Just consider, the majesty of rivers?

There was an old man with a goat,
An amusing old man with a goat,
        The man with the goat
        Was a man with a goat
That interesting old man with a goat.

There once was this doctor called Jones,
A medical doctor, named Jones,
        And this Doctor Jones
        This doctor, this Jones,
Was a crazy old doctor called Jones.

As well as writing limericks, Ted Lear has left us with some of the most enchanting nonsense verse in the language.

The Pibbledy-Pobbledy Man

When the Yonghy Bonghy's singly fat
On the coast of the Fimbly Far,
And the beauteous Lady Jingly's hat
Looks up at the evening star.
He weeps alone on the shingly shore,
He pumpkinly goes for a walk,
Drinks his marsala through calico straws,
He haveth a runcible dork.

Rapidly numerous,
Vapidly humorous,
He mourns with a sweet guitar,
The wonderful pussy is loved by the owl
Who feels a complete galah.
When the Yonghy Bonghy has lost his way,
The birds make a nest in his beard,
He sits in the afternoon tea tree,
And regrets it is just as he feared.

William McGonigall

William McGonigall was once a familiar sight around the Universities, where he wrote and performed in the bardic manner. Although largely ignored at that time, he later headed a Government steering committee on Arts funding and in this capacity set up The Australian Literature Board. To this day their policy reflects all essential aspects of William McGonigall.

The Westgate Bridge Disaster

I'm extremely sorry to have to say,
A terrible thing happened the other day,
On the otherwise beautiful Port Phillip Bay,
An enormous but unspecified degree of destruction
Has pole-axed the bridge which was under construction,
And a number of souls have been spirited away.

Oh appalling thing! Ye girders immersed!
The Westgate Bridge is completely burst,
Such dreadful events could ne'er be rehearsed,
How distressing for the perished, honour their memory,
Some of them probably served with Montgomery,
Although of all their experiences this would be the worst.

It was said by experts that the bridge was alright,
But boy were the experts in for a fright,
When bits of the aforementioned sank out of sight,
With a crash and a hideous graunching sound!
Many fragments on the sea-bed later were found,
And the Westgate Bridge was in a desperate plight.

The Rev. George Gilfillan saw the bridge begin to sway,
A popular and highly moral man which no-one can
    gainsay,
And for the emergency telephone he did reach without
    delay,
And he nobly sought assistance from the suitably qualified,
'Our gracious span is in grave peril. Do something!' he
    cried,
Which the people of Melbourne remember to this very day.

The immortal William Shakespeare is needed at such
    times,
Whose understanding of tragedy is surpassing fine,
Such as for instance certain bits of Othello which are truly
    most sublime,
Only he this catastrophe in its magnitude so vast,
Could describe although ironically he's dead and in the
    past,
A loss which the people of Melbourne will mourn for a
    very long time.

A pall hangs over Melbourne which can ne'er be blown
    away,
And which no sensible person has any reason to gainsay,
And the pall is particularly prominent over Port Phillip
    Bay,
Where a combination of dreadful weather
And a lack of adequate bracing together,
Brought such tragic results on October 15th 1970 which
    was not a happy day.

Emmy-Lou Dickinson

Film devotees will remember Emmy-Lou as an extra in 'Witness' (directed by fellow-Australian Peter Weir) but it is as a poet that she is best known to date. A very quiet person, she lives alone near Lakes Entrance and speaks only to small children on her mother's side.

Are you anybody? I'm not either,
Come over here before somebody finds us,
We'll hide so everyone fails to notice
That nobody knows where we are.

Imagine being someone, Yikes!
How appalling — like a toad —
Puffing up one's throat all day
For a lot of other warts.

Exhilaration is the coming
Of the mariner uphill,
Through the wood — along the ridge —
To the utmost peak —

From the land as if for the first time
The sailor watches the storm
With the godlike perspective
Afforded by the recognition
Of form.

What is? Is this?
Can this be? If not this —
Then what? Something else?
Nothing?
Death perhaps?
Death is not nothing —
Death is something — it happens —
It follows something else —
Or nothing —
Or something other than either —
Possibly this.

Preciousness is the essential aspect
Of all the things that are precious;
I'm pretty sure this is right —
It is certainly a lovely idea.

To wither away of boredom
With only the bee to consider
Is my choice — my right — my life —
My start — my end — my God.

I fear the small —
The slight — the brief —
The large I can deal with —
But the speck — the infinity
Inside the merest particle —
Is enormous.

The Flashing Gyre.

I roam with the ~~old~~ men, piping their song,
The moon-road and troubled engaged in a reel,
The careless white hair of them streaming along
As they dance in the tops of the trees,
The loopy old men, the wild-eyed and punching,
Who better than know their ~~faint~~ hearts beat?
For old men know old women,
And old women have dreams at their ~~foot~~ feet.

I mistook the quickening fiddler's hand
For the swan-beat of wings ~~passing~~ by,
For old men are merry when roaring with fire
And birds and old women lament with the sky
Or why if the wandering wind-driven MacCool
And Brigit held hands at the fair
Should not old men salmon-leap into the ditch
Remembering glances that sang on the air?

the end

Yeats' handwritten draft. Original on quarto typewriting paper. (Reproduced by kind permission of Yeats' family.)

Walter Burley Yeats

Often referred to as the authentic voice of Tasmania, Walter Burley Yeats was elected Senator in 1922, and won the Nobel Prize for Shearing in 1931, 1932 and 1933.

The Flashing Gyre

I run with the old men, piping their song,
The moon-mad and troubled engaged in a reel,
The careless white hair of them streaming along,
As they dance in the tops of the trees,
The loopy old men, the wild-eyed and punching,
Who better than know their hearts beat?
For old men know of old women,
And old women have dreams at their feet.

I mistook the quickening fiddler's hand
For the swan-beat of wings passing by,
For old men are merry when roaring with fire,
And birds and old women lament with the sky.
Or why if the wandering wind-dried MacCool
And Brigid hold hands at the Hobart Fair
Should not old men salmon-leap into the ditch,
Remembering glances that sang on the air?

Teddy Bentley

The inventor of the detective novel, Teddy is best remembered for the four-line construction known as Cheerios, so called for no good reason.

Cheerios

Alan Border,
Sequestered himself down the order,
And seldom, even during a rout,
Went out.

The thing about Malcolm Fraser,
Was the authority of his old school blazer,
The pants, it should not be forgotten,
He wore less often.

Reactions to Keating are funny,
And indexed completely to money.
Those with lots like him best,
Nonetheless.

Jems Choice

Jems is one of Tasmania's best known exports. He left Hobart with Enid Carbuncle before the First World War and never went back. He got a job teaching English in Brisbane and began work on his novels. His first works were heavily criticised in the Tasmanian press and he spent the rest of his life writing one that no one would understand.

The Ballad of Jasper O'Reilly

Nearly recovered we are blathered here today
In the flight-path of Himself
Dijon disbanding this woman in howdy-doodiedom
Do you (insert your trained leer Mr Earwicker)
Take Anna Livia to be or not
To be your lawful dreaded life?
Eyedew.
Under you, Anna Livia, talk this man
(Insert your train here Mr Wicker)
To be your awful bedded strife?
Adieu.
If anybum nose often impedimenta
Speak nowra four of a whole jaw-piece.

Unpack the voluminous dative case and lay out
The suit my grammar left me the mardi da,
The mither of the fither sun and noilly pratt
Parse the photo correction, lookit the faces,
Theres Dante, dont minchinbury legion,
Seether man in the hat? Boylan for the wife he is
Cant get enough off her always warm in the bed.

This hears Molly wither clothiers on
And thesis the dress under where just under there
The underwear sur prize sur prize
All stand while we observe the holy trinity
Come come now Mr Deedless do not toy with the caught
Put them on a good behaviour bond
Ant twatted he say when he touched you my child?
Pig in your porter butters this seat taken?
Nature of Inquiry;
Genuine, searching, passibly dooble onton,
Character of response;
Fellatious, mollified, deeply touched,
Dr Ring will free you now three cheers no waiting.

The fiddle he diddled the dada did
He middled the little La Scalas id
Belittled the riddle the fathers hid
Skedaddled and addled the sorters of
The muddle was on for supporters of
And all of the Murraying waters of
The hurry and worrying waters of
Lights going
Fights going
Sights going
All of the sons and daughters of
The trouble enchanted ought is off
For all of the martyred daughters of
Night.

R.A.C.V. Milne

Essayist, poet and commercial traveller, R.A.C.V. Milne wrote a number of verses for children. His best-known works are still read today.

The Dog's Breakfast

Bob asked Neil,
And Neil asked Susan,
Do you think that we could rustle up support for the I.D.?
Neil spoke to Susan,
Susan said 'Certainly,
I'll go about the countryside and see what I can see.'

So Susan she took her leave,
And went down to Tasmania,
And told them they were ignorant
And stupid as could be,
And they didn't understand,
And the government would have its way,
The card was coming in and everybody should agree.

But the people said they didn't,
And they couldn't and they wouldn't,
And they shouldn't, it was rotten,
But that even if they did,
Who was going to have access
To the facts about the taxes?
How could anybody guarantee complete security?

So Susan went to Neil,
She told him of the news,
She told him how the people felt
And how she'd been accused
Of invading of the privacy
Attempting to dehumanise
And tamper with the sanctity of individual rights.

Susan told Neil,
And Neil went to Bob,
Bob said 'Bother',
Or words to that effect,
He fulminated briefly,
Said that what he wanted chiefly
Was to do the thing for which
He'd asked the people to elect him.

But John put the card to sleep,
Establishing his fame,
And great was the rejoicing
Of the folk who thought the same,
But we're left with the position
That in keeping with tradition
It's the rich to which the pleasure
And the poor to whom the blame.

Obviousness

Rob Rob Bobbity Bobbity James Lee Hawke M.P.
Took great care of his image because he was quick to see
That if you are photographed standing with blokes
Whose boats do well on the sea,
Millions of voters will fail to notice
The blokes will be charging a fee.

Kahlihliji Bran

Kahlihliji was a migrant to Australia, settling in Sydney from Lebanon. He had studied sculpture under Rodin but at that time nobody in Australia had heard of either Rodin or sculpture. Kahlihliji became a visionary.

The Half-Yearly Prophet

And a Punter came forth, which was not unusual, and said Speak to us of Race 5 at Randwick.
And he answered and said:
Goodness me, is that the time?
People of Moron, I say to you, Wisdom is not in others. It is in ourselves. We are not others. Other people are. We are us. And yet they are not Them. They are merely an Us which does not include anyone here. Any questions so far?
The world is a seamless cloth. Take shelter in it but do not expect it to fit.
Love and Understanding are but winds that bear the spirit.
Love may be given but cannot be taken.
Understanding can be neither given nor taken but is the string in the bow of Life.
We are not Us either, incidentally, I should make this clear. Just a small one thanks.
Everything is its own opposite.
Paradox is that which is not paradoxical.
Only the living know death. Only the dead are living.
Only the lonely, dum dum dum dumdedoowah, know the way I feel tonight. Jameson's if they've got it.

A cow has many windows, but only one rudder.
Reason is a tool. Try to remember where you left it.
If you are rich and would give, give not your money.
The poor know nought of money. Give them of yourself.
A smile, a pat on the head, something of that order.
And he beckoned to the pilot.
I must take rest for a time, he said, possibly on Venus.
And he was gone.

William Esther Williams

Williams was a doctor whose interest in Imagist poetry helped him greatly in his work. Very interested in nature, especially, like Marianne More, in the pantheistic resonance of great big animals.

The Carnival

Why is it that every year
On remote coastlines
Labour leaders
Beach themselves?
Whole schools of them,
Apparently healthy Labour leaders
Thousands of miles off course and stranded,
Spume drifting from their tragic holes.

Why do they do it?
Is it not knowing where they are going?
Or is it guilt over where they have been?
There is no more futile prospect in nature
Than ordinary folk with flippers and buckets
Working urgently in the deepness of the shore
To turn the stricken Labour leaders around
Before nightfall.

Pinko Brooke

Pinko Brooke, whose origins are uncertain, had no formal education and began working as a drover at eleven. He was typical of a generation of young men who went away to the First World War; Brookie, like so many others, did not come home. He was killed in the attack on Nieppe Forest in August 1915, two days after writing 'The Soldier'.

The Soldier

If I should die think only this of me
That there's a little bit of Ballarat in Belgium
And some Bowral and some Nowra and a fair degree of
    Cowra
And perhaps a dash of in behind the back of Wendoree.

T.S. (Tabby Serious) Eliot

Tabby Serious Eliot was born in Mallacoota but went to school and university in Melbourne, qualifying as a surveyor in 1915. Among his other works is 'Old Ponce's Book of Practical Webbers'.

The Love Song of J. Arthur Perpend

Let us go then, you and I,
While there's still time to read and classify,
Measuring the margins on the little fey barometer
That marks the calibrations of our talk.

In the room the women come and go
Despite what I read in the papers.

Old is what I seem increasingly to be,
Tobacco-tranced in time I watch the sea,
It was a dark and stormy old pyjama cord
That lashed me to my dream of others moored,
There followed soft a moment put on hold
With a wind without a rug against the cold
And someone, call it someone, up on an elbow,
For argument's sake, might say,
'You have missed the point,
You have completely missed the point'.

In the room the women come and go
But not, perhaps regrettably, with me.

CAVITY

The Accounting Cat

Liquidity's a mystery; it's very rarely seen,
It strikes and then is gone again, its getaway is clean,
And despite forensic evidence and great deductive flair,
The conclusion's inescapable, Liquidity's not there!

Liquidity, Liquidity, there's nothing like liquidity,
Its presence gives you confidence, its absence is timidity,
You own perhaps a property, you own perhaps a share,
But once you've lost your credit card, Liquidity's not
there!
Your understated opulence inheres in what you wear,
But in the end you face the fact, Liquidity's not there!

Liquidity's a nifty term, it's business talk for cash,
It's money not tied up in things or hoovered in the crash,
Investments may return amounts of staggering obscenity,
The vastness of your holdings may explain your great
serenity,
In publishing, to take the case of either of the Fabers,
A warehouse full of Larkin and The Bumper Book of
Neighbours,
Is very well, and when they sell, will satisfy the editors,
But not much use, in real terms, when dealing with the
creditors.

Liquidity, Liquidity, there's nothing like Liquidity,
The glint of actual duckets brings respect and dipthelidity,
It's likely to self-immolate on contact with the air,
Say 'Raffle' in a crowded room; Liquidity's not there!

In the conduct of a company (proprietary limited)
There's always a suspicion that the system's
maladministered,
In proper corporate planning you allow a little spare,
But when you need the wherewithal, Liquidity's not there!

Liquidity, Liquidity, there's nothing like Liquidity,
In purely economic terms it constitutes validity,
I wish I had a pound for every credit millionaire,
Who completely failed to register, LIQUIDITY WASN'T THERE!
When reputations tumble and the search is on for clues,
(I might mention humpo-bumpo, I might mention
drinkie-poos)
There's a suspect who can prove he was in Lima at the
time,
They can't catch him, he's the brilliant Scarlet
Pimpernel of crime!

DOROTHY PARKINSON

Writer of bitter-sweet reviews and short stories. Member of the famous Alqongwoin 'Drunks' group.

THE STORY SO FAR

Poland works nicely,
Chad's going well,
Burma's precisely
Successful as hell,
Haiti is lovely,
This time of year,
Sudan is just darling,
Thank God for Zaire,
Chile's a dish,
Brazil is a dream,
South Africa's bliss,
And Iran is a scream.
Go lease a car,
Go purchase a suit,
Everything's ducky,
And I'm King Canute.

b.b.hummings

b.b. drove an ambulance in the First World War and was mistakenly imprisoned by the French. He never fully recovered and returned to Australia in some confusion. Tragically, he did not know he wrote poetry. He thought it was 'just a lot of nonsense'.

74

this bit

foll
owe
db
y

this bit

and

then

this bit
over here

n
seasons change and leaves go w
u o
p d
or

coolman;unmanuncool
(nothing)

?

huh?

Ogden Gnash

Ogden Gnash was perhaps the best known of the Perth poets.

Pardon Me Madam But Is That Mandible On A Leash Or What?

Of all the tenets mentioned in discussions about levity,
By far the most important and the best of them is brevity,
So Shakespeare and Railway Timetables and instruction
manuals in foreign languages apart,
Be, of all literary forms, most suspicious of the poem which
is almost entirely parenthetical and despite whose
Towards More Picturesque Speech homely
cleverness in the Norman Rockwell manner, leaves
you wondering whether you've left the gas on and
whether you've got to throw another six to start.

Sir Don Betjeman

Don represented Victoria in cricket, tennis, golf and car-spotting. Wrote 'The Shell Guide' for Victorian motorists. He worked in television during the 1960s and released the names of every architect employed on the Albury-Wodonga Development Project. He lived in Malvern and was King of Moomba in 1972.

Another Subaltern's Wedding

When I saw you at the service,
Didn't have the guts to speak,
Should have, can't think why I didn't,
Perfect oppo up the creek.

Back at the Reception Centre,
All those lovely downy thighs,
Waitress asked me if I'd like some,
Herbert Adams party pies.

After bouncy hot Gay Gordon,
You and I became a pair,
What a thrill! Joy unconfined!
At Berlei stockists everywhere.

In the carpark, Jowett Javelin,
Triumph of post-war design,
Hugged the road to Mount Eliza,
Hard beside the Frankston line.

Past the Dendy, through Moorabbin,
Near St Kilda Football Ground,
Mentone, Mordialloc, Carrum,
Seaford next and homeward bound.

Off the Melway briefly poppet,
Up the Old Road, rally style,
Let me, dear, into your secret,
Silken delta of the Nile.

Advice To Chaps From Parents

Whatever you do, don't touch yourself down there,
And if you want to know something, ask me,
Or if I'm not available, a prayer,
For God's sake don't ask Uncle Dorothy.

STEWIE SMITH

Stewie spent most of her working life as a secretary, although she is better known for her poetry, as is frequently the case in Australia.

FURTHER THOUGHTS ABOUT THE PERSON FROM PORLOCK

There ought to be a Monument
Put up in the public square,
To honour the memory of the
Unknown Person from Porlock,
Who paid the supreme sacrifice
That certain others might live.

They have got it wrong
The Coleridge people,
What they have got is wrong,
The Person from Porlock has been
Wickedly misunderstood,
It is too late now of course,
It is too late.

I yearn for the second coming
Of the Person from Porlock,
I anticipate the epiphany and have left instructions
That I am to be disturbed
The moment my thoughts are assembled.
If somebody else does not do it,
One of these frosty Fridays
I might just do it myself.

Who are these blessed people
Who complain their ideas won't come?
Don't they know what it is like?
May we have their names please?
They ought to unfurl a crimson runner,
They ought to welcome Him,
He is Our Saviour you see,
For he brings the precious gift
Of interruption,
World not without end,
Amen.

I can see I'm not helping,
You do not want to hear this, I know,
But how, other than with distress
Are we to respond to our thoughts?
Imagine not having an imagination.
We are trapped, don't you see?
The way to heaven is hell.

W.H. Auding

Wisty Huge Auding published his first collection, 'Poems', in 1928, followed by 'A Whole Lot More' in 1932 and 'When We Were Very Old' in 1960. He died in 1968, 1971, and again in 1973.

Muse of Bauxite

About Telecom they were never wrong,
The Old Masters, how prescient they were
About existential services;
How well they knew the mundane brutality of increasing
charges for items which don't exist,
How, while oafs deliberate, holding money
Up to the light, agreeing it should be described
Not as a profit but as an operating surplus,
There always must be, bleak-faced, random and frantic,
Victims, trying to make urgent calls on public phones
dangling
From walls in a twisted piss-smelling tardis,
And in the distance a man sits on a park-bench,
Explaining to his grandchild the merits of competition.

In Nolan's *Ned Kelly* series, for instance, how everyone's
face
Is either hidden or green; hidden, encased
In metal, in uniform, angled, straight and hard,
Or green, and how, when Scanlon is shot from his horse
And falls, he falls up,
Unsurprised, a bystander,
He's thinking 'Dearie me,
Another ballsup'.

Louis 'The Lip' MacNeice

Recruited from Northern Tasmania in 1925, MacNeice became one of the mainstays of Australian verse between the wars.

What I Did In The Holidays

Section IX

In a week I shall return to the University
And begin again the selection of anecdotes,
Revealing the ageless to the briefly young,
Explaining the dead to the living,
Arranging the facts in a circle and playing
Simon says The Glory of Greece.
Balance your chair on the bookcase,
Study the dust in a shaft of light,
And listen to the familiar stories,
Nod with the names, salute the heroes,
The paragons, the exceptions that prove the rules;
Plato, Diogenes, Alcibiades,
The Thracian vases, Delphi on a clear day,
Liking the Spartans less because we
Could never do that with our young.
Observe the neat morals, the perfect natural laws,
The foundations of modern justice:
At least one foot must be on the floor
While towing Hector around the walls of Troy,
Gentleman are requested to wear a jacket
During the putting out of eyes,
Lotuses should not be consumed in the upstairs bedrooms,
Persons tied to rocks and women with uncontrollable
boxes

May be charged accordingly.
A code not so much to be used as admired,
To know the classical, the ordered, the decent,
From the random pillage of the horde,
And to decide whether I am part of the one
Or simply at odds with the other,
And to pick at the seam of this discipline,
Which presents the apotheosis as the norm,
Which dresses the writers, the dramatists,
The hypocrites, the philosophers and the lads
Who drew right-angles in the sand with sticks,
As the standard, the usual things
Done in the usual way.

And I think myself of the blockheads, the pimps,
The hired thugs and the imposters,
The mountebanks with imported sandals,
And the developer's brother-in-law
Who spoke in the Agora securing the right
To fatten some olive groves mentioned in Hesiod
And open a π shop.

Flagpole Music

It's no go the tight-head prop, it's no go the hooker,
Wait till the bloody thing's put in straight and review it for
 The New Yorker,
Wystan Hugh went up to Iceland in a shower of rain,
Addressed an epistle as Juan's apostle and buggered a dog
 on a chain,

It's no go the Willie Away, it's no go the droppie,
Run it and draw the defence in the centre and stick up a
 kick if it's sloppy,

Oliver Gogarty went for a swim and put in a personal best,
Presented the Liffey with plenty of swans and did what he
 could for the rest,
The appendectification of Yeats, the Celtification of John,
The Mulliganising of Martello Jim, the Newdigate Prize
 having gone,

It's no go the half-time score, it's no go relaxing,
They'll come out of there like a bull at a gate after getting a
 boot in the jacksie,

Roger Casement looking to drive, splitting the men in the
covers,
Caught in the lovely Republic of Irony, strung up as high
as his lovers,
Bernard Shaw went to visit himself, sequestered away in a
castle,
And F.E. Smith, should it please the court, fellated the
late King's arsehole,

And it's no go Hotel du Lac, it's no go the Amis,
The Booker is rigged and as boring as shit and the
publishers want to be famous,

It's no go the final effort, it's no go the gumption,
It's into the showers and out of the steam and off to the
after-match function,

It's no go the Wittgenstein, it's no go linguistics,
It's no go the sober pricks, quickly becoming the
pissed-pricks,
It's no go the Cabaret, it's no go the ball-gown,
All we want is a bang in the dark and a mate and bottle of
fall-down,
It's no go the juxtapose, it's no go the finger,
Ladies and gentlemen join with me now in formally
thanking the singer.

Dylan Thompson

Martyr to the turps, Dylan Thompson frequently woke in unfamiliar circumstances and attempted to catch the speech rhythms of the sea.

A Child's Christmas in Warrnambool

One Christmas was so like another in those years around the sea town corner now, that I can never remember whether it was 106 degrees in 1953 or whether it was 103 degrees in 1956. All the Christmases roll into one down the wave-roaring salt-squinting years of yesterboy. My hand goes into the fridge of imperishable memory and out come: salads and sunburn lotions, the brief exuberant hiss of beer being opened and the laugh of wet-haired youths around a Zepher 6, the smell of insect repellent and eucalyptus and the distant constant slowly listless bang of the flywire door. And resting on a formica altar, waiting for Ron, the biggest Pav in the world; a magic Pav, a cut-and-come-again Pav for all the children in all the towns across the wide brown bee-humming trout-fit sheep-rich two-horse country.

And the Aunts. Always the aunts. In the kitchen on the black-and-white photographed beach of the past, playing out the rope to a shared childhood, caught in the undertow and drifting.

And the Uncles, wondering sometimes why they weren't each other, coming around the letterbox to an attacking field in the Test match and being driven handsomely by some middle-order nephew, skipping down the vowel-flattening pitch and putting the ball into the tent-flaps on the first bounce of puberty.

Larry Parkin

Larry, a crumpled and charming deep-voiced man who had normally just got off a train, was a member of 'The Outfit', a group which dominated post war Australian verse. He had sex in 1963, before many of you were born.

Mr Peacock

'This was Mr Peacock's room. He dwelt
In deepest fantasy, you never knew
Exactly who he was or how he felt,
As leader or with bullet-hole in shoe.

He might be someone else, De Gaulle, St John,
It changed so often we became confused,
He'd plan to win a prize, embark thereon,
Then have it offered to him and refuse.

This is where he slept, just over here,
Though what he did at night, you'd never know,
The sunlamps just provided a veneer,
Long haul, he thought embalming was the go.

The chair is where he'd leave his favourite book,
Was most particular it not be moved,
We heard it rumoured once he took a look,
But unsubstantiated; can't be proved.

The night he did the deed he got back late,
He told us, around 3.30, maybe 4,
"The lads and I have just farewelled a mate.
Farewelled him from the 42nd floor."

He's gone from here of course, but he'll be back,
We'll be asked if we can house an ageing turk,
He's smart enough to give himself the sack,
If it looks as if he'll have to do some work.'

This Be The Chorus

They piss you off, your kids, I guess
They're got at by these Freudian shits,
As if it's our fault they're a mess.
After all I've done for tits.

Vern Scanlon

Very big in the local RSL in Mackay, Vern has long been concerned with the major themes of twentieth century writing; violence, the RSL, and Mackay.

Standing Orders

Some nights, after lights out,
I slip round to Bluey Nesbitt's,
And after a few snifters,
We turn back the German advance.

Pulling the pins from six bread-rolls
With our teeth, we hurl them
Into the shed where moonlight assures us
A crack Panzer Division Victa Utility
Has been moved up on to our flank.

It's dirty work
But someone's got to do it.

Dream

All those women who have not got
Beautiful breasts and great legs
And lovely soft sweet-smelling hair
One pace forward Betty Grable where the bloody hell do
you think you're going?

Sylvia Blath

Born in Mosman, Sylvia wrote about illness and death. She sometimes did it ironically but always, behind all the fun, were illness and death. She called it a day in 1963.

Self Defence

You do no soft, you do no soft,
No more the old soft shoe,
In which I once delighted when you
Danced upon my cradle, as I
Annexed the Sedatenland.

I clapped my partly German hand,
On my partly Polish one,
Just like in real life,
And when you came home, achtung!
You wiped your boots on my face.

In the shadows you ordered away the lives
Of all of us black Jewish Poles,
Your daughter you condemned
To the oven, subtle in leather,
Der Ofen! Schnell!

Pig brute fatso bastard,
Shit bugger bum fuck poos,
Daddy daddy I'm through, Hello?
Germaine I can hardly hear you,
This is a very bad line.

Margaret Attwood

Margaret comes from the bush up near Cooma and writes almost everything produced in Cooma. As well as her poetry she has produced a number of novels, mainly about Cooma.

Everyone Dances

Look Janet look.

See Janet run.

Why is Janet running?

More particularly why is she running from John?

Can anyone think of a reason why she might be running towards Peter?

How many people have spotted Janet's mistake?

Janet wants to be a nurse when she grows up.
Janet wants to help people.
Janet is a people person.

Oliver wants to be a doctor and cure diseases.
Oliver is too young to know what doctors really do.

Oliver and Janet attain their majorities and meet at a party at Peter's house.
They fall in love over half a bottle of wine and a Raoul Dufy print and they leave in Oliver's powerful thrusting sports car.

Oliver turns out to be a complete arsehole of course. How many of you noticed me setting him up?

Janet runs into John at a Woody Allen movie and although John is almost as boring as the Woody Allen movie, he offers stability and reasonable genetic stock. They marry and Janet has two babies almost immediately.

Janet loves her children but something is missing. After a time of wonder, she identifies the missing element as Peter. She meets Peter at a series of rendezvous so as not to alert Peter's wife. This works well and John is not at all suspicious since he is not that sort of person. He is the sort of person who has been corking his secretary, the lissome Fiona, for nearly four years.

Janet and Peter eventually find their affair becoming slightly less magical so they give it away and go back to civilian life. Peter makes a confession to his wife in which he pretends to recognise her value and blames himself in a manner which makes her feel responsible.

Janet drinks like a fish and St John the Martyr feels justified in manipulating Fiona.

Can we all see the people Janet helped?

Can Janet see?

Look Janet Look.

Index of First Lines